I0569973

Learning LOL

Welcome to my class about Daily Vocabulary Flashcards! My name is Professor Charlie, and I am so excited to show you all the fun things my assistant and I have been learning. My assistant is my mom, and she is super helpful! She reads all of the research we do together out loud, takes me for walks when it is time for a break, finds yummy treats for the both of us to share, and also does all the typing since she has fingers and thumbs, and I only have paws, and the most important thing of all, she gives the best belly rubs. My job is to give her fun ideas to look up, to keep her warm with cuddles, and to try not to bark at the mailman. I make no promises about the last one. We make a really great team!

Last week, I was helping my assistant wrap a birthday present in our office because it was my brother Smokey's birthday. She was sitting on the ground and asked me to get a pair of scissors and some scotch tape for her off the desk. I know I have heard these words before as I scratched behind my ear, but I am still learning to speak English. Barkinese is my first language, and English is my second, so sometimes I still get confused. My assistant is so patient and kind because she teaches me how to speak and understand English, so I knew I needed to help her find these objects and be a good boy. I went over to the desk, stood on my hind legs, and put my front paws on the desk. I looked at the different things we had on our desk.

I knew some of these objects right away, like pen, paper clips, pencil, and lined paper, but the scissors and the scotch tape were a little more tricky. I looked for a few seconds and grabbed two things I thought were correct. I walked back over to her, placed the objects beside her, and smiled shyly. She looked down and smiled. She told me I grabbed the scissors, which was amazing, but I got a stapler, not the scotch tape. I said I was sorry and put my head in her lap. My mom, sorry, I mean, my assistant, told me it was okay and told me to look up. I slowly lifted my head and saw that she was smiling at me.

She then took each cheek in her hands, gave me a big kiss on the forehead, and gave me chin scratches. She told me she knew I tried my best and that we all make mistakes. It was hard to learn another language, and she was so proud of how hard I was working. After a few minutes of belly rubs and telling me what a good boy I was, we went to the desk, found the scotch tape, and finished wrapping Smokey's gift.

At the end of the day, when it was time to relax on our cozy sofa, my assistant brought us our favorite snack (peanut butter & apples), and we snuggled under the blankets. After a few minutes, I asked her if she could help me with something. Of course, she said yes with excitement. I asked her if we could make different flashcards of the objects around the house and in our office. I wanted to practice all of the daily vocabulary words that I could. I told my assistant I could also start teaching Smokey some English! He only speaks Barkinese right now because he is new to our family. He is smart and scrappy, so I know he will talk to my assistant in English soon. But most of all, I want to practice to help my assistant as she helps me. She said this was an amazing idea! Then, at the very same moment, we looked at each other with huge smiles on our faces and said, "We should make a book for our pup pals so they can learn with us!" After that, we stared at each other for a quick second, then let out a huge laugh! After we got ourselves under control, we went to work and wrote not 1 but 2 different daily vocabulary word flashcard books.

I had so much fun running around the house and the office, asking, "What's this?" over and over and over and over again. And I'm sure my assistant had just as much fun as I did. When we were all done with our flashcards, we showed them to Smokey, and he did a super job for a beginner. We told him we left **blank flashcards** under the different topics so he could make his own flashcards. He is a good drawer, so I can't wait to see what pictures he will draw and the words he will practice. He was a little sad that he didn't get everything right the first time, but I told him it was okay, and I didn't get some words correct the first time, either. After I told him I would help him practice, which made him so happy to hear, his curly tail began to wag very fast.

Over the next few days, Professor Charlie and Smokey would walk around the house and match the flashcards to the real objects around the house. This way, they could practice different words all day long. Smokey had some trouble with how to pronounce some words. Thankfully, Smokey and Professor Charlie have their assistant Tara to help them, but if you have trouble pronouncing a word, don't worry, my pup pal. Ask a grown-up for help or ask if you can search the word's pronunciation online in the search bar. Never go online without permission. Manners and safety first! I hope you enjoy our book, new pup pal. We will see you for your next lesson!

Tara & Charlie Morrish

**Photos by
Scarlet Morrish**

Professor Charlie   **Smokey**

Where learning language online is fun!

We want to thank you, from the bottom of our paws to the tips of our ears, for buying our book! We hope you enjoyed reading it as much as we enjoyed writing and researching it. We are also excited to share that, coming soon, you can join us on our website. Here, you can view all your favorite topics with videos, maps, and pictures, along with interactive worksheets and flashcards. To make entering the classroom easier, scan the QR code, but remember to ask your grown-up first before going on the internet. See you there!

Where learning language online is fun!

Learning About Everything Around You!

Table of Contents

Alphabet A-L

Learning About Everything Around You!

© 2023

Aa

Bb

Aa

Bb

Cc

Cc

Dd

Dd

Apples	**Alligator**
Bananas	**Bear**
Cucumber	**Cat**
Donuts	**Dog**

Ee

Ee

Ff

Ff

Gg

Gg

Hh

Hh

Eggs	**Elephant**
Figs	**Fish**
Grapes	**Goat**
Honey	**Horse**

Ii 	Ii 
Jj 	Jj 
Kk 	Kk 
Ll 	Ll 

Ice Cream	**Igloos**
Jam or Jelly	**Jellyfish**
Kiwi	**Kangaroo**
Lemon	**Lion**

Animal Body Parts 1

Learning About Everything Around You!

Shell	**Shell**
Feathers	**Feathers**
Claws	**Claws**
Webbed Feet	**Webbed Feet**

Antennae	**Antennae**
Fin	**Fin**
Fur	**Fur**
Trunk	**Trunk**

4 Hooves	**1 Hoof**
Talons	**Talons**
Wings	**Wings**

Animals and Babies 1

Learning About Everything Around You!

Cow and Calf	Wolf and Pup
Hen and Chicks	Duck and Ducklings
Elephant and Calf	Bear and Cubs
Dog and Puppy	Cheetah and Cubs

Frog and Tadpole	**Cat and Kittens**

© 2023

The Bathroom 1

Learning About Everything Around You!

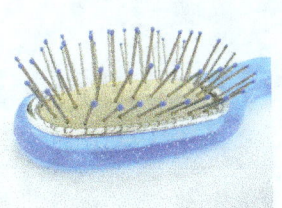

Toilet Paper Roll	**Shower Curtain**
Toothbrush Holder	**Soap Dish**
Faucet	**Shower Liner**
Medicine Cabinet	**Hair Brush**

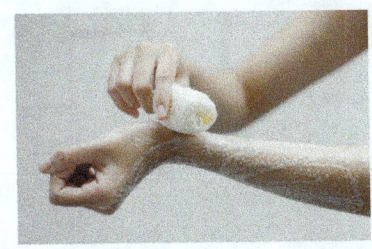

Shampoo and Conditioner	**Blow Dryer or Hair Dryer**
Bar Soap	**Toilet or Potty**
Body Wash	**Liquid Soap**
	Luffa

The Bedroom 1

Learning About Everything Around You!

Pillows	**Comforter**
Sheets	**Sleeping Bag**
Mattress	**Decorative Pillows**
Vanity	**Toys**

Lamp	**Throw Blanket**
	Shoe Rack

The Body 1

Learning About Everything Around You!

© 2023

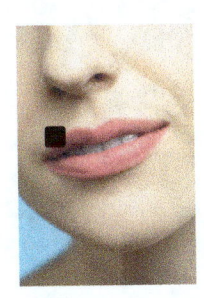 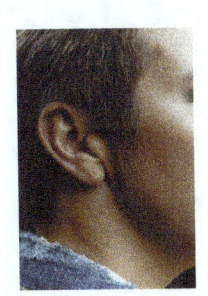

Ear	**Lips**
Hands	**Knee**
Arm	**Cheeks**
Eye Lashes	**Neck**

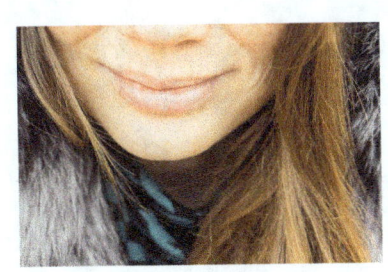

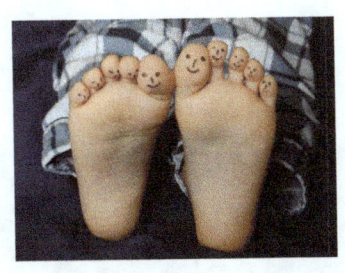

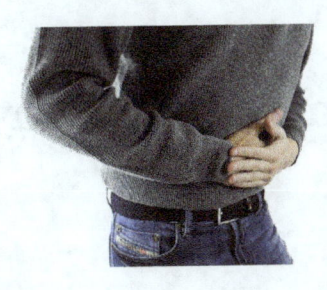

© 2023

Mouth	**Finger Nails**
Eyes	**10 Toes**
8 Fingers	**2 Thumbs**
1 Tooth & 2 Teeth	**Stomach, Tummy, Belly**

**Belly Button
or Navel**

Clothes 1

Learning About Everything Around You!

© 2023

Jumpsuit	**Shorts**
Jacket	**Sweater**
T-Shirt	**Tank Top**
Sun Hat	**Dress**

Skirt	Romper
Jeans	Overalls
Swimming Trunks or Swimming Shorts	Pants
	Bathing Suit or Swimming Suit

Fruits 1

Learning About Everything Around You!

© 2023

Kiwi	**Passion Fruit**
Cantaloupe	**Apples**
Raspberry	**Pineapple**
Grapefruit	**Pomegranate**

Lime	**Peach**
Pear	**Orange**
Strawberry	**Lychee**

The House 1

Learning About Everything Around You!

© 2023

Tent	Apartment
Dining Room	**Office**
Townhouse	**Kitchen**
Cabin	**Castle**

Bedroom	Bathroom
House	Living Room

© 2023

The Kitchen 1

Learning About Everything Around You!

© 2023

Sink	**Fork**
Bowl	**Spoons**
Oven	**Colander**
Refrigerator or Fridge	**Stove**

Cupboard or Cabinets	**Faucet**
Dishwasher	**Counter Top**
Glass or Cup	**Plate**

The Living Room 1

Learning About Everything Around You!

Throw Blanket	**Throw Pillow**
Sectional	**Coffee Table**
Arm Chair	**Light Switch**
Curtains	**Candle**

Loveseat	**Window**
Sofa or Couch	**Side Table or End Table**
	Carpet or Rug

Numbers 1-10

Learning About Everything Around You!

© 2023

© 2023

Two Cats	**One Star**
Four Eggs	**Three Dogs**
Six Penguins	**Five Monkeys**
Eight Colored Pencils	**Seven Flowers**

9

10

1

2

3

4

5

6

Ten Balloons	Nine Candles
Two	**One**
Four	**Three**
Six	**Five**

7	8
9	10

Eight	Seven
Ten	Nine

The Office 1

Learning About Everything Around You!

Books	**Desk**
Desktop Computer	**Dictionary**
Office Chair	**Headset or Headphones**
Eraser	**Pencil**

Lined Paper	**Pencil Sharpener**
Stapler	**Crayons**
Calendar	**Colored Pencils**
	Permanent Marker

Shapes & Colors 1

Learning About Everything Around You!

Green	**Rectangle**
Purple	**Star**
White	**Diamond**
Pink	**Heart**

Black	**Oval**
Brown	**Moon or Crescent**
Yellow	**Triangle**
Orange	**Arrow**

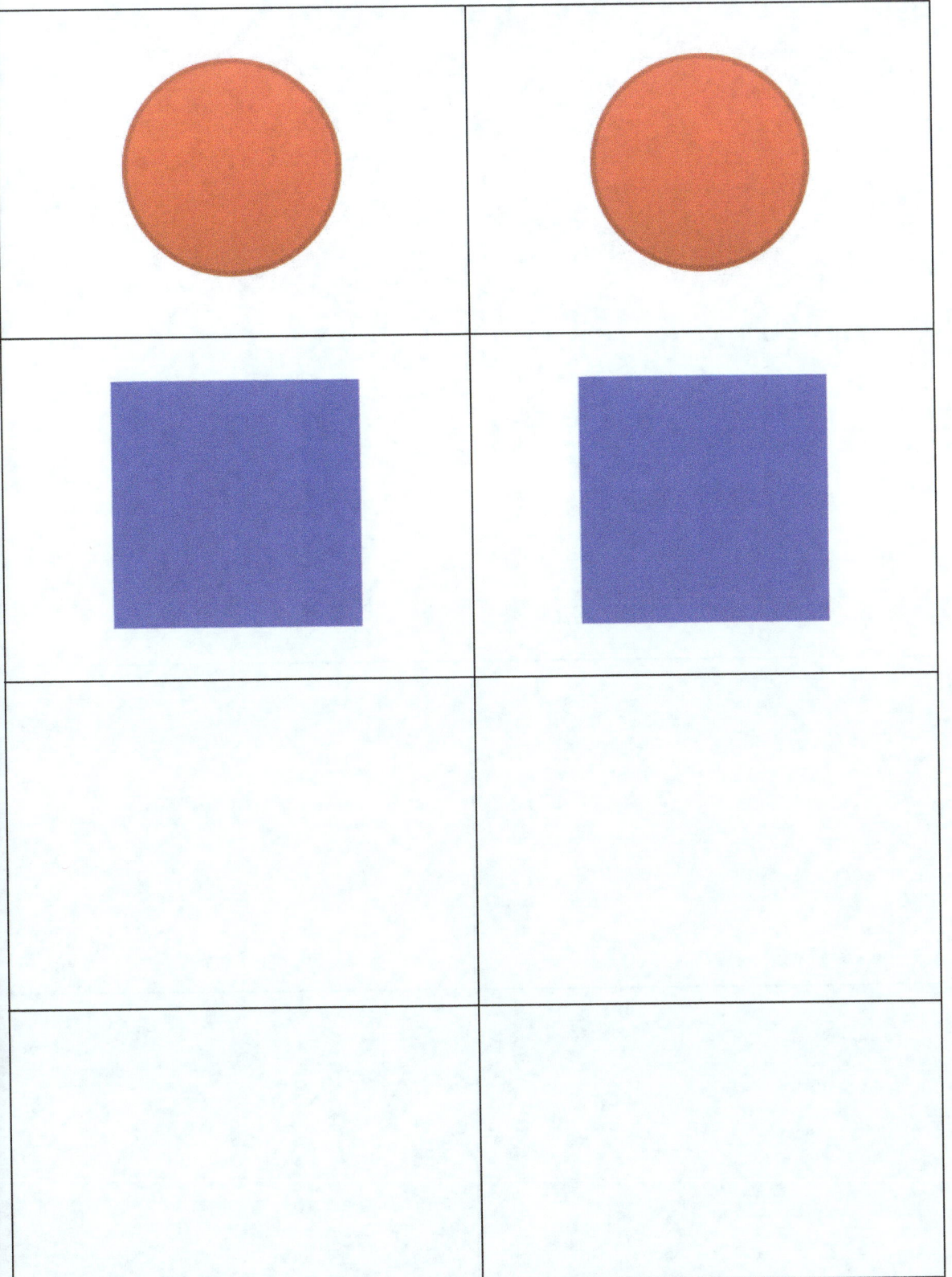

Red	**Circle**
Blue	**Square**

Sports 1

Learning About Everything Around You!

© 2023

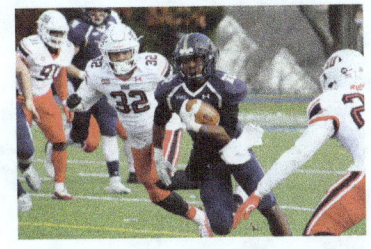

Skiing	**Volleyball**
Table Tennis or Ping Pong	**Baseball**
Bowling	**American Football**
Basketball	**Golf**

Tennis	**Bobsledding**
Wrestling	**Badminton**
Boxing	**Soccer or Football**

Vegetables 1

Learning About Everything Around You!

Pea Pod	**Peas**
Green Beans	**Broccoli**
Corn on the Cob	**Corn Kernels**
Peppers	**Potatoes**

Cucumber	Zucchini
Brussel Sprouts	**Red Cabbage**
Squash	**Onion**
	Carrots

Vehicles 1

Learning About Everything Around You!

Sail Boat	**Airplane**
Canoe	**RV or Recreational Vehicle**
Cruise Ship	**Boat**
Car	**Taxi or Cab**

	SUV or **Sports Utility Vehicle**
Helicopter	
School Bus	**Pickup Truck**
City Bus	**Trolley**

Weather 1

Learning About Everything Around You!

(season)

© 2023

Snow	Thermometer
Tornado	Hurricane, Typhoon, or Cyclone
Winter	Celsius and Fahrenheit
Clouds	Flood

(season)

Rain	**Avalanche**
Blizzard	**Dew**
Icicle	**Rainbow**
	Summer

Where learning language online is fun!

Learning About Everything Around You!

Don't forget to check out our other books, Animals Around the World, Winter Olympics, Creative Writing, Places Around the World, and Pronunciations.

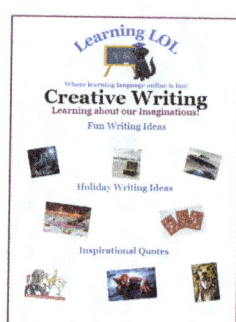

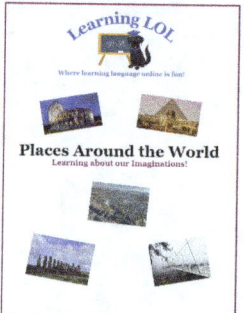

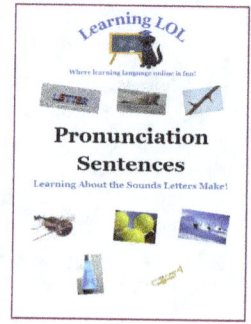

Make Your Own Flashcards

 © 2023

© 2023

Learninglol.com

www.ingramcontent.com/pod-product-compliance
Lightning Source LLC
Chambersburg PA
CBHW080844120626
46553CB00009B/2556